D0906110

THE FARM

FARM KIDS

Ann Larkin Hansen
ABDO & Daughters

Published by Abdo & Daughters, 4940 Viking Drive, Suite 622, Edina, Minnesota 55435.

Copyright © 1996 by Abdo Consulting Group, Inc., Pentagon Tower, P.O. Box 36036, Minneapolis, Minnesota 55435 USA. International copyrights reserved in all countries. No part of this book may be reproduced in any form without written permission from the publisher.

Printed in the United States.

Cover Photo credits: Peter Arnold, Inc.
Interior Photo credits: Peter Arnold, Inc.

Edited by Julie Berg

Library of Congress Cataloging-in-Publication Data

Hansen, Ann Larkin.
    Farm Kids / Ann Larkin Hansen.
      p. cm. -- (The Farm)
    Includes index.
    Summary: Describes aspects of life on the farm such as the abundance of space, the need for safety, the importance of work, and the value of clubs, projects, and fairs.
    ISBN 1-56239-623-4
    1. Farm life--Juvenile literature. 2. Children--Juvenile literature [1. Farm life.] I. Title. II. Series: Hansen, Ann Larkin. Farm.
    S519.H375 1996   96-11120
    305.23'0973'091734--dc20   CIP
                                                       AC

About the author

Ann Larkin Hansen has a degree in history from the University of St. Thomas in St. Paul, Minnesota. She currently lives with her husband and three boys on a farm in northern Wisconsin, where they raise beef cattle, chickens, and assorted other animals.

Contents

Lots and Lots
of Space

Farm kids don't just have backyards to play in, they have whole farms. There is room to dig holes, build forts, and ride ponies and **four-wheelers**. With no city lights close by, the stars are very bright.

Farm kids see sunrises and sunsets. They build bonfires and burn them under a full moon. They watch plants and animals grow. There is always something to learn and see on a farm.

Opposite page:
Farm kids loading up
the compost wagon.

How Many Kids?

Out of 75 million kids in America, only about one million live on farms in the United States. Another two million live in small towns and **rural** areas.

In many ways, farm kids are just like other children. They like to play Nintendo and go shopping. They do homework and play on sports teams. They like to hang out with their friends. But in some ways, life for farm kids is very different.

Opposite page:
These farm kids
are gathering eggs.

Farm Safety

Farming is one of the most dangerous jobs in America. Each year, accidents with machinery and animals kill or injure many farmers and farm kids. Farm kids must learn the basic rules of farm safety at a very early age.

Farm kids know never to go alone into a **pen** or **pasture** with adult male animals. They never get between a mother animal and her young. They know never to work on machinery unless it is turned off. They let their parents know where they are.

Opposite page:
This farm kid knows
better than to climb
inside a pig's pen.

Learning to Work

Farm kids are an important part of the farm business. There is a shortage of farm workers, so parents need their children's help. By the time they are in grade school, most kids have jobs around the farm. They might be in charge of feeding calves or lambs. They learn to grease machinery and stack hay.

Farm kids also learn they must work until the work is done. They can't quit just because they are tired or hungry. They work hard, and their parents are proud of them.

Opposite page:
One chore for farm kids
is feeding the calves.

How Farm Kids Play

Farm kids don't work all the time. There is plenty of time to play. Farm kids go fishing, fly kites, and build treeforts. They ride their bikes down the **farm roads**, and build treasure boxes in the shop. Many kids like to snowmobile, waterski, and ride **minibikes**.

Farm kids like to relax, too. They lie on their backs in the **pasture** and watch the clouds. They capture crickets and fireflies. They poke sticks into anthills.

Opposite page:
Farm kids have
plenty of fun, too!

School

Schools in **rural** areas are often smaller than city schools. There are fewer new kids and fewer children who move away. In such a small group, everyone learns to get along with the others.

Farm kids usually have long bus rides. In northern states, schools can close for days because of snowstorms. Farm kids also have some different sports. In many states, they can join the **rodeo** team!

Opposite page:
Two farm boys at a rodeo.

Clubs for Farm Kids

In the early part of this century, **youth** clubs were organized in Iowa by Albert B. Graham. He began by having corn-growing contests for kids. Soon there were more contests and projects. In 1914, Congress established **4H** clubs across the country.

The 4H clubs believe that children learn by doing. Each club member picks projects to work on that year. They can choose from projects in animal science, **mechanical** sciences, **environmental** education, home and health, and many others.

Opposite page:
A farm girl who raises
calves for 4H club.

4H Projects

Beginning in the fall, **4H** kids work on their projects for a year. Some kids raise calves. They must figure out feed **rations**. They teach the calf to lead with a rope, and to stand still for brushing. They must weigh the calf regularly to see how it is growing.

Other children may choose art projects. During the year they practice different ways to draw and paint. They also may work on projects like cooking, sewing, model rockets, or woodworking. Adults help them fill out project records.

Opposite page:
A 4H project making
elaborate scarecrows.

Fairs

Sometime in the second half of summer, farm kids pack up their projects and take them to the fair. Usually a special **4H** building displays all the birdhouses, bug collections, garden vegetables, and other projects made by 4H kids. There are special shows to judge 4H calves, pigs, sheep, and other farm animals.

After the judging, farm kids like to have fun on the rides and stuff themselves with fair food. They wander around with their friends and have a good time.

Opposite page:
This farm girl's calf won
a blue ribbon at a county fair.

Other Clubs
and Programs

When farm kids get a little older, there are other activities for them to do. Many join Future Farmers Of America (FFA). They learn how to judge cattle and **soils**. They may also do projects, such as raising **pheasants** and ducks.

All farm kids who want to drive a tractor must be at least 14 years old and take a **tractor safety course**. Kids who want to hunt must take **hunter education**.

Opposite page:
A farm kid who raises
geese and ducks.

Farm Kids and Their Parents

Farmers work at home, and usually their kids help. So, farm kids spend more time with their parents than city kids.

Farm kids listen to their parents talk about the farm over dinner. They learn about the problems and plans for the farm. They also learn to think things over, and help decide what to do.

Farm kids learn to be responsible and to spot problems. This way, they become an important part of the farm business.

These farm kids help their dad prepare dinner.

What Farm Kids Know

Farm kids learn early that machinery breaks. They learn that animals get sick and die. They learn that crops can be lost to bad weather, bugs, or weeds. They learn that problems are a normal part of life.

Farm kids know that you can fix most problems and cure most animals. They also know that space, fresh air, hard playing, and all the work of farming is what makes it great to be a farm kid!

Farm kids have plenty of time to play.

Glossary

environmental (en-vie-run-MEN-tull)—the study of the Earth's land, air, and water.

4H—an organization of children; the h's stand for head, heart, hands, and health.

farm roads—the dirt roads in fields used for moving farm machinery to and from sheds and fields. These are not public roads.

four-wheeler—another name for an all-terrain vehicle, or ATV; an open, balloon-tired small vehicle.

hunter education—this course is a federal requirement for young hunters. Age requirements vary from state to state. Contact your county extension office for more information.

mechanical (muh-CAN-ih-kull)—relating to machinery or tools.

minibikes—miniature motorcycles.

pasture (PASS-chur)—a large, fenced area for grazing animals.

pen—a small, enclosed area for animals.

pheasants (FEZZ-ants)—a bird about the size of a chicken, usually raised for release into the wild.

rations (RASH-uns)—to supply an animal with food.

rodeo (ROW-dee-oh)—a sport that evolved from cowboy days. There are many events, including bronco and bull riding, and steer roping.

rural (RUR-ull)—country.

soil (SOY-ull)—part of the Earth's surface in which plants grow; dirt.

tractor safety course—this course is a federal requirement for any child between the ages of 14 and 16 if they wish to operate machinery on any farm except that of their parents.

youth—a young person.

Further Information

For more information about farms, check out the following books:

Beard, D.C. *The American Boy's Handy Book.* Boston: David R. Godine, 1983 (original texts published in 1882 by Charles Scribner's Sons).

Beard, Lina and Adelia. *The American Girl's Handy Book.* Boston: David R. Godine, 1987 (original texts published in 1887 by Charles Scribner's Sons).

Both of these books are loaded with games, projects, plans, and ideas for country kids. Much of the information is dated, but still enjoyable.

For more information on 4H, contact your county agricultural extension office. 4H has traditionally been considered a rural organization, but is now available everywhere.

My thanks to Don Dukerschein, 4H Youth Development Agent for Chippewa County, Wisconsin, for his help with this book.

Thanks also to my own "farm kids," Nick, Phil and Joe.

Index